(c) Copyright 2025, Freedom Philosophy. Cover background image generated by AI.

All rights reserved.

No part of this publication may be reproduced, distributed, or transmitted in any form, without the prior written permission of the publisher. Small parts of this work may be referenced and quoted under under fair use legislation, provided it is clearly attributed to the author.

Bulk orders may be placed by contacting the author:
Tel/SMS: +61 416243242
Online: www.freedomphilosophy.life
Printed in Australia

Publisher's Cataloging-in-Publication data
Visser-Marchant, Cornelis PJ
Divine Healing: a practical course for personal application / Cor Visser-Marchant.
89p. 14 x 21cm.
Legal deposit with archives of National Library of Australia and State Library of Queensland. Free or discounted deposits with other libraries considered upon written request.

ISBN 978-0-6450743-6-9 (Paperback)
1. Spirituality and Faith - Philosophy - Spiritual Philosophy.
2. Religion - Christianity - Spiritual Christianity.
3. Healing - Prayer - Spiritual Healing.

First Edition

Unless indicated otherwise, scripture taken from the King James Version. Public Domain.
Where indicated scripture references are from the New King James Version®. (NKJV) Copyright © 1982 by Thomas Nelson. Used by permission. All rights reserved.
Where indicated scripture taken from the NEW AMERICAN STANDARD BIBLE® (NASB). Copyright © 1960, 1962, 1963, 1968, 1971, 1972, 1973, 1975, 1977 by The Lockman Foundation. Used by permission. www.lockman.org
Where indicated scripture quoted from The Holy Bible from Ancient Eastern Text (LAMSA), translated by George M. Lamsa, © 1933, Harper One. Used by permission.

Divine Healing

a practical course for personal application

Written by

Cor Visser-Marchant

For Sally

My gratitude and dedication goes out to the Divine Source: Jehovah God; the great I AM and the only true teacher and healer from whom our life and wisdom comes. It is He who gives us the authority to overcome and endure.

"Behold, I give you the authority to trample on serpents and scorpions, and over all the power of the enemy, and nothing shall by any means hurt you."
Luke 10:19 NKJV

Why this book?

There are many wonderful and angelic people in the world and that becomes no more apparent than when you truly need some help. Even as strong believing Christians, we often fail to seek or accept help, perhaps even considering ourselves unworthy of it. Moreover, while we intellectually know that miraculous healing is possible, we tend to attribute this ability only to Jesus Christ and His biblical disciples described in the scriptures. However, we must not gloss over the granting of His Authority to us over anything false and evil. The sacred scriptures are clear that through our faith healing can and does indeed occur. This authority is not merely granted to church leaders or so called 'gurus', but is open to everyone equally - if only you are able and willing to receive it.

We were reminded by our brothers and sisters in China, while we were there for my wife's treatment as part of her battle with Stage IV colorectal cancer. The overwhelming love and support we received from total strangers was awe-inspiring and the Chinese Swedenborgian community renewed our hope and belief in Divine intervention through miraculous healing. We had several healing prayer sessions with sister Ying and given a bi-lingual pdf with 30 days worth of healing scriptures and confirmations. Things did start to turn around and this inspired me to make a similar course available, with some context, in this book form. Putting this into a book, makes it more readily available to anyone and enables ready portability (put it beside the bed, highlight sections, make notes and share reading in a group setting).

It is my hope that the context and the overall selection and ordering of the material assists with the effectiveness of your healing journey. I have incorporated some quotes and references from other teachings, because they compliment and underscore the promise we find in The Holy Bible. To work within the limitations of copyright laws, I selected a variety of scriptures from the most accurate English translations available.

Finally, this book supports the recipients inner work and healing process. Given the chance and time you can see the Divine Healing power at work. Please share this with anyone who is in need of healing.

Table of Content

Why this book?	... vi
The Promise	... 9
Divine Source and Creation	... 14
- The Divine Source	... 15
- The Spiritual World	... 19
- The Human Mind	... 20
- The Natural World	... 22
- The Body	... 24
- The Environment	... 27
- Our Regeneration	... 29
- Summary	... 32
The Healing Process	... 34
How to use this book	... 35
Daily Healing Sessions	... 37
The Word	... 756
Prayer	... 77
What we cannot control	... 78
Reference Sources	... lxxxiv

The Promise

Before stepping into the first day's prayer and focus affirmations, it is important to establish the foundation of faith and belief in the testimonies found in the Sacred Scriptures.

Once I show you the validity of the promise of healing found in The Holy Bible, I will explain the process and nature of creation and reality, supported by the scriptures, modern science and ancient wisdom alike. I reaffirm the universal nature of reality - knowledge which was common in ancient times, and even understood later by occasional wise masters, but lost to modern society. However, first things first.

It may seem obvious, but is easily ignored or forgotten: the Divine is infinite and so not confined by time and space. While we have been able to observe His power in the natural, as described in the scriptures, He always was and always will be. For this reason God is called Jehovah, which means: "Is, was, (coming into) being.", as we can also read in Revelation:

"Grace be to you, and peace, from him who is, and who was, and who is to come."
Revelation 1:4 LAMSA

And

"I am Alpha and Omega, the beginning and the ending says the LORD God, who is, and who was, and who is to come, the Almighty."
Revelation 1:8 LAMSA

And

> "..and the Word was God. …..All things were made through Him, and without Him nothing was made that was made. He was in the world, and the world was made through Him."
>
> John 1:1,3,10 NKJV

And, if this was not yet sufficient to show that the Word - the expression and visible creation from the Divine - is immutable and has always been there unchangable.

> "Jesus Christ is the same yesterday, today, and forever."
>
> Hebrews 13:8 NKJV

This means that the authority and power of God with us today is **NO** different than it was *in the beginning.*

The universe (ie the external reality we experience), which exists only on account of the immutable creative force from the Divine (the same force that also operates through us), is not under the control or power of the natural and illusory nature of our external world. It is therefore also logical to conclude that nothing in the natural world has any spiritual power. Therefore we read:

> "You are of God, little children, and have overcome them, because He who is in you is greater than he who is in the world."
>
> 1 John 4:4 NKJV

And

> "These things I have spoken to you, that in Me you may have peace. In the world you will have tribulation; but be of good cheer, I have overcome the world."
>
> John 16:33 NKJV

Some may think it is only on account of a petition, a request that we submit in form of what is commonly called prayer, that we join a spiritual triage queue where our requests may be honoured if we are deemed righteous and needy enough. For example due to scriptures like this:

> "Is anyone among you sick? Let him call for the elders of the church, and let them pray over him, anointing him with oil in the name of the Lord. And the prayer of faith will save the sick, and the Lord will raise him up. And if he has committed sins, he will be forgiven. Confess your trespasses to one another, and pray for one another, that you may be healed. The effective, fervent prayer of a righteous man avails much."
>
> James 5:14-16 NKJV

This is why many think they are a victim or dependent on the prayers and blessings of others. However, nothing could be further from the truth. It should by now be obvious that none of the usual characteristics of us fallible humans, such as anger, discrimination, judgement and favouritism apply to God, who is more like a constant life force. Not unlike the way the sun blankets us all indiscriminately with light and warmth.

I like to remind you that healing is available to everyone - not only the elders of a church - and yes, this includes **YOU!** We all - you my dear reader included - have been given this authority as co-contributors in the creation process originating from the Divine. If you're still not certain about the truth that the Source is within you:

> "the kingdom of God is within you."
>
> Luke 17:21

which grants everything you truly want:

"Let it be as you desire."

Matthew 15:28

and has given you all authority and power:

"Behold, I give you the authority to trample on serpents and scorpions, and over all the power of the enemy, and nothing shall by any means hurt you."

Luke 10:19 NKJV

It is not that this power comes from our own efforts or believing in natural laws and scientific fields like medicine only. No, the power, authority and creative life force originates only from the Divine. It is the Spirit that lives and gives life only, while we are merely channels and vessels. Or to say it otherwise, we are rooted in Him as vine:

"I AM the vine, you the branches; he who is remaining in Me, and I in him, this one bears much fruit, because apart from Me you are not able to do anything."

John 15:5 LAMSA

Elsewhere too we are asked to look to the infinite, rather than be trapped by believing in the illusory limitations of the natural/external world we experience. We just need to get out of the way and work in harmony with reality as it objectively manifests.

"But Jesus looked at them and said, 'With men it is impossible, but not with God; for with God all things are possible.'"

Mark 10:27 NKJV

When we believe, have faith and so trust and know the reality that God exists. When we know that it is only the spiritual realm (or to say it differently, the realm of the mind) that drives and creates the external (natural) world. When we acknowledge that our healing starts within - the domain of the Spirit. Then we will be able to experience miracles:

> *"And Jesus went about all Galilee, teaching in their synagogues, preaching the gospel of the kingdom, and healing all kinds of sickness and all kinds of disease among the people."*
> Matthew 4:23 NKJV

Divine Source and Creation

*I*t is well recognised by anyone with some level of spiritual insight and wisdom that there is a single intelligent consciousness that is the source of all life and reality as it objectively manifests. I also highlight this in my book *New Perspectives*. This knowledge is not limited to Christianity and The Holy Bible, but also inherent in Judaism, Islam, Sikhism, Some forms of Hinduism, Zoroastrianism, Bahai, et cetera and many (if not most) indigenous spiritual traditions, and can sincerely be considered ancient sacred knowledge. It is therefore important that we start there:

> *"In the beginning God created the heavens and the earth."*
>
> *Genesis 1 NASB*

In order for healing to occur, you may not need to understand any more, but for some to truly accept and believe that it is the spiritual or unseen reality that creates and manifests the external and experiential (senses based) realm, I include this chapter. This is so you may know, without ambiguity, that creation and therefore the root cause of any disease originates in the spiritual realm - or to say it with a different word - the mind! It is the same thing!

The mind directly manifests as result of the will - what is loved. We exists on account of the unconditional love that is Source, who goes by many names like: Jehovah God, The Lord, The Word. We manifest our own external experience of life from the quality of our character (what we love). To say it in a different way, the external world is a reflection of the internal. We are co-creators and through the choices we make subconsciously choose our own circumstances.

Let us have a look at what various sacred texts tell us about the creation process. We will look at this in order of the process itself, which can be summarised as:

1. The Divine Source (a priori)
2. The Spiritual World (world of causation)
3. The Human Mind (intermediary)
4. The Earth and Natural World (world of effect)
5. The Human Body (health effect)
6. Environment (reflection of inner state)
7. Return Path (regeneration)

The Divine Source

While the core aspects of the Divine Consciousness, being Love itself and Wisdom itself - the single Source of Reality - does not need much elaboration, I still like to share these verses from the Bible to add some baseline context:

> "To us there is one God, the Father, from whom comes every thing and by whom we live; and one LORD Jesus Christ, by whom are all things, and we by him."
>
> 1 Corinthians 8:6 LAMSA

> "In the beginning was the Word... and without Him nothing was made..."
>
> John 1:1,3 NKJV

> "God is love."
>
> 1 John 4:8

> "By the word of the Lord were the heavens made,"
>
> Psalm 33:6

> "You created all things, And by Your will they exist and were created."
>
> Revelation 4:11 NKJV

Sadly the false idea of three distinct personas has infected the minds of Christians, but if you read carefully and think logically about God's nature, you will see that the Divine Love (or Will) is the Life force referred to as 'Father' - the unseen without form. It has expression and form through Divine Wisdom - referred to as The Word or 'Son'. The activity proceeding from Source is referred to as 'Holy Spirit'. In reality, they are not separate or even distinguishable in actuality, but innate aspects of the Infinite One.

If you are familiar with the Bible, you will know there are many, many more verses similar to those shared above. Great reading on this topic can also be found in the revelations of Emanuel Swedenborg (1688-1772), who shares that:

> "God is Love itself and Wisdom itself."
>
> Divine Love and Wisdom 28-32

In his most famous work *Heaven and Hell* he reiterates that The Word is not only the Light (literally in the spiritual world), but the essence of Him (the Father) is Love (which is the life of all):

> "The Lord is the Sun of Heaven... whose essence is Love"
>
> Heaven and Hell 116–118

In my book *New Perspectives* I discuss the concept of love, which I recommend you read, as this concept is commonly misunderstood. In Hinduism too, we have some beautiful examples of a Conscious Creator from which reality

Divine Source and Creation

originates: a pure consciousness:

> *"There is nothing higher than Me... all this universe is strung on Me like pearls on a thread."*
> Bhagavad Gītā 7.7

> *"I am the source of all spiritual and material worlds."*
> Bhagavad Gītā 10.8

> *"The Supreme is 'the beginningless, the supreme beyond existence and nonexistence.'"*
> Bhagavad Gītā 13:13

All these show the Divine as underlying reality behind both spiritual and natural worlds. Not surprisingly this is echoed in Islamic sacred text too:

> *"Allah is the Light of the heavens and the earth."*
> Qur'ān 24:35

> *"His throne extends over the heavens and the earth."*
> Qur'ān 2:255

> *"He is the First and the Last, the Outward and the Inward."*
> Qur'ān 57:3

It should not be a suprise to anyone that there is a clear shared understanding across cultures and time that God is the origin and sustaining reality of all levels of existence. Outside of relatively modern religious context, we see the Great Spirit / Creator as the Source of life and order in all the Indigenous or First Nations traditions.

The Australian Aboriginals are possibly the longest continuous surviving culture known today with archeological evidence of their presence on the Australian continent going back 45,000 years. Their concept of a Creator-being who brings order to land, life, and law, is called *Baiame*.

The native Sioux (Lakota/Teton) in the Americas call it *Wakȟáŋ Tȟáŋka*; the Great Mystery, source of all.

Even in Budhist teachings, not known for acknowledging a single autonomous Deity, we can find a clear concept of a single source, unmutable consciousness:

> *"There is, monks, an unborn, unbecome, unmade, unconditioned. ... therefore you do know an escape from the born, become, made, and conditioned."*
>
> *Udāna 8.3*

Other examples I recommend reading include:
- Taoism: Tao Te Ching chapters 1 and 25;
- Confucianism: Doctrine of the Mean; and
- Sikhism: Siri Guru Granth Sahib 1-5, 5-1, 294-12.

It is then not unexpected that all of these religions and spiritual traditions, besides Christianity, provide us with the fundamental law, or original instruction if you prefer (represented in the book of *Genesis* by rules given to Adam and Eve and by Moses bringing down from the mountain the stone tablets written by the finger of God), that we humans must align ourselves with the order of Creation - the *Divine Order* or *Divine Providence* as Swedenborg describes. Non-alignment is the cause of all suffering. Let me repeat and highlight that:

Non-alignment with the Divine Order of creation is the cause of all suffering.

The most well known, most singularly comprehensive and most culturally pervasive rule, present in one form or another in almost all religions, is:

> *"In everything, therefore, treat people the same way you want them to treat you, for this is the Law and the Prophets."*
>
> *Matthew 7:12 NASB*

Living according to this fundamental law requires us to align our heart and mind and act according to what we love and believe to be true - without selfishness and hypocrisy. Therefore, it is important for us to understand the nature of this Divine Order and nature of reality to avoid and/or correct any possible suffering.

The Spiritual World

Once you understand that everything originates from a single infinite source, which is consciousness (mind) and also called the Great Spirit, it is clear that it is the spirit (mind) that precedes and gives effect to the natural. Or to say it differently, the natural only exists because of the spiritual reality that enables and manifests it. We read in scripture:

> *"It is the Spirit who gives life; the flesh provides no benefit"*
>
> *John 6:63 NASB*

> *"the worlds were framed by the word of God, so that the things which are seen came to be from those which are not seen."*
>
> *Hebrews 11:3 LAMSA*

> *"All things were created through Him and for Him."*
>
> *Colossians 1:16 NKJV*

What I wish to highlight here is that the natural world (ie the realm of our physical and sense based experience) is not created separately and continues to operate autonomously, which is what deists believe. No, it is clear that the spiritual is what actively creates and sustains the natural.

Swedenborg puts it like this:

> *"The things that are in nature are nothing but effects; their causes are in the spiritual world. ... the effect ceases when the cause ceases"*
> Arcana Coelestia 5711 (Clowes)

In the Bhagavad Gītā we read that the physical/material is non-existent, whereas the soul is eternal. In other words, physicality is an illusion observed and manifested by the spirit.

> *"Those who are seers of the truth have concluded that of the nonexistent [the material body] there is no endurance and of the eternal [the soul] there is no change. This they have concluded by studying the nature of both."*
> Bhagavad Gītā 2:16

In Australian Aboriginal spirituality, the concept of dreamtime asserts an unseen causal realm underlying visible nature. In other words, creation arises from a non-material spiritual dimension that continuously shapes the physical world.

In his book *Divine Love and Wisdom*, Emanuel Swedenborg explains that all of creation relates to Love and Wisdom (aspects of the Divine) and so correspond to the extend they reflect the image of it. Correspondence is how the spiritual manifests the physical and physical reflects the spiritual. (eg see sections 52, 83)

The Human Mind

You will likely have heard the truism that we are not physical beings having a spiritual experience, but spiritual beings having a physical experience. It must obviously be true if the natural is dead and non-existent without the mind that creates it.

What may be less obvious, but becomes clear with some consideration, is that when we say spirit or mind, they are synonymous terms. Consciousness is another term that can be used and while these terms predominantly focus on the understanding part (ie image of Divine Wisdom), it cannot be separated from the affectionate part (ie image of Divine Love). We are soul and spirit (mind), being the thoughts and intents of the heart. The following verses offer some example:

> *"For the word of God is living ... piercing ... soul and spirit, ... the thoughts and intents of the heart."*
> *Hebrews 4:12 NKJV*

> *"And do not be conformed to this world, but be transformed by the renewing of your mind."*
> *Romans 12:2 NASB*

And

> *"..put on the new self who is being renewed to a true knowledge according to the image of the One who created him."*
> *Colossians 3:10 NASB*

And again

> *"..you are to be renewed in the spirit of your minds,"*
> *Ephesians 4:23 NASB*

So the human mind is the interface between soul and body. Or as Swedenborg describes the mind **is** the spirit, while the body is its external reflection. It is not until we change what is within - the internal, that our external experience changes. This is because the external reflects the eternal: the natural is an image of the spiritual (ie what is internal).

The Qur'ān also acknowledges something similar:

> "Allah does not change the condition of a people until they change what is in themselves."
>
> Qur'ān 13:11

In the Māori traditional spirituality *Wairua* (spirit) and *Hinengaro* (mind) shape one's presence and experience.

Collectively pervasive sacred traditions and texts show the mind as a sacred interface between the spiritual and natural worlds.

In other words, what we have read shows that, in the image of our Creator, we are (our) mind, which quality - nature or character - is the result of what we love and believe to be true - the affections and thoughts we 'own'.

The Natural World

The natural world, therefore, is thus an effect. A material plane receiving influx from, and so being caused by, the spiritual. We may often gloss over it and continue to buy into the idea that the physical world is distinct, real and somehow separate from the spiritual, because for the most this is the way we have 'experienced' it growing up. This too is the reason why many think spirituality is an activity or intellectual process (belief), but in *New Perspectives* I explain why that idea is false. The realm of the mind (spirit) is what gives effect (cause) to the natural (ie sense based) realm.

> *"Thy will be done, as in heaven so on earth."*
> Matthew 6:10 LAMSA

> *"that which may be known of God is manifested to them for God has revealed it unto them. For, from the very creation of the world, the invisible things of God have been clearly seen and understood by his creations,"*
> Romans 1:19-20 LAMSA

Emanuel Swedenborg gives us a great summary and explanation of what is commonly known a the 'Law of Correspondence'.

> *"Everything in the universe answers to something in us...everything in the animal kingdom, ... everything in the plant kingdom, and ... with everything in the mineral kingdom."*
> Divine Love and Wisdom 52 (Ager)

and

> *"The whole natural world corresponds to the spiritual world, and not merely the natural world in general, but also every particular of it; and as a consequence everything in the natural world that springs from the spiritual world is called a correspondent. It must be understood that the natural world springs from and has permanent existence from the spiritual world, precisely like an effect from its effecting cause"*
> Heaven and Hell 89 (Ager)

However this is also known, or referred to, by alternative terms such as: the principle of "*as within, so without*", or "*as *above, so below*", having ancient origins in Hermetic philosophy. According to *Wikipedia*, the writings attributed to Greek Deity Hermes Trismegistus, referred to as the Hermetica, were produced over a period spanning c. 300 BC – 1200 BC: Hermes is also thought to be the revered prophet Idrīs in Muslim and Bahá'í theology.

As an interesting side note, in Homeopathy it is well recognised that healing occurs from the inside out and that the root cause originates on the energetic meta-physical level of the vital life force (think spirit by another name).

The Bhagavad Gītā tells us that Lord Krishna is above the natural and that many are deluded or fooled by the illusion of the natural world. In reality all modes of energy are manifested by His energy, including the material world. However, these are within Him and Lord Krishna is not subject to these lower energies, but inexhaustible. (See section 7:12-15)

Taking a leaf from African indigenous religion; In Nigeria, the Yoruba Ifá tradition, the physical world is seen as a reflection of the spiritual world, a concept that emphasizes the interconnectedness of all existence. Their monotheistic centuries old view holds that the earthly realm (*Aiye*) is an extension of the spiritual realm (*Orun*) and that divine and ancestral forces continuously influence and communicate with the living.

This connection means that the material world is infused with spiritual energy, and a person's actions in the physical world have direct spiritual consequences. They believe that the earthly realm is a mirror of the spiritual cosmos. In other words, the natural world is not separate, but reflects (or embodies) the spiritual realm.

To put it into simpler words: there is a common view, especially in the more ancient spiritual traditions, that thought manifests (creates) the 'reality' we experience.

The Body

This brings us to the obvious conclusion and significant realisation that the physical body we often think of as being us is also part of the natural world. Therefore our body too is a direct effect and ultimate manifestation of our mind (ie spirit). Just as the natural world has correspondence to the realm of the mind, so has our 'physical body' direct correspondence to the inner life of our mind.

The difference is that the natural world is the total effect of our collective spiritual influence, whereas our body is the direct result of our own spirit. The most direct effect can be observed nearest to us personally (our bodies, our home, our garden) reflecting our own states. The less direct in the effect can our influence be observed with more shared environments, reflecting more collective states.

Many of the well known dramatic stories of healing in scripture reveal a direct link of a physical outcome resulting from a spiritual change. For example:

> "And they brought to him a paralytic ..., and he said to the paralytic, Have courage, my son; your sins have been forgiven. .... Arise, take up your quilt-bed, and go to your home. And he rose up and went to his home."
> Matthew 9:2,6-7 LAMSA

The apostle John here seems to indicate a direct link between the health of the body and the health of the soul:

> "I pray that in all respects you may prosper and be in good health, just as your soul prospers."
> 3 John 1:2 NASB

And in proverbs another example tying the nature of our character to the life of our body:

> "A sound heart is the life of the flesh."
>
> Proverbs 14:30

And even more clearly:

> *Incline your ear to my sayings.*
> *They are not to escape from your sight;*
> *Keep them in the midst of your heart.*
> *For they are life to those who find them,*
> *And healing to all their body.*
> *Watch over your heart with all diligence,*
> *For from it flow the springs of life.*
>
> Proverbs 4:20-23 NASB

Emanuel Swedenborg's revelations go into great detail about the nature of the spiritual world (heaven and hell) and the importance of our inner reformation. He makes it clear in *Arcana Coelestia* (translated as Secrets of Heaven) - a spiritual commentary on Genesis and Exodus over 8 volumes (Latin):

> "All diseases in man have correspondence with the spiritual world; for whatever in universal nature has not correspondence with the spiritual world cannot exist, having no cause from which to exist, consequently from which to subsist."
>
> Arcana Coelestia 5711 (Clowes)

and

> "diseases ... correspond to the yearnings and passions of the lower mind, which are also their origins; for the origins of diseases are, in general, intemperance, luxury of various kinds, mere bodily pleasures, as also feelings of envy, hatred, revenge, lewdness, and the like, which

> destroy man's interiors; and when these are destroyed
> the exteriors suffer, and drag man into disease, and so
> into death"
>
> Arcana Coelestia 5712 (Clowes)

Also from *True Christian Religion*:

> "it is the man's form, which is induced upon him by the
> states of his life"
>
> True Christian Religion 366 (Ager)

In a different way, the Bhagavad Gītā outlines how food preferences and other behaviour are linked to our motivations and that ultimately unhealthy/unbalanced spiritual motivations produce physical harm. (eg 17:5-9)

In the natural we can observe stress raising cortisol and thus inflammation, affecting our overall metabolic health. We can observe the results of poor eating and lifestyle habits. We can even observe the nocebo and placebo effects - scientific studies qualified it to affecting 74% of the outcome - being purely the effect of belief/thought.

However all of these are observable outworkings of a fundamental law: the spiritual (ie realm of the mind) is what gives cause and effect to the natural.

The eternal gives effect to the external. As such disease, health, beauty, vitality etc. all mirror/reflect/project our spiritual states.

To say it in a plain way: what we love, think and believe affects our physical health - AND the world around us!

In the ancient traditions of Chinese medicine (TCM) and Ayurvedic healing it is accepted that the body reflects an imbalance in spirit/mind (qi, prana). In homeopathic medicine, the mental symptoms reflect the deepest and most important causal aspect to treat. In north American indigenous medicine they believe that disease arises when one is "out of balance" with spirit, community, and land, while in Australian aboriginal healing illness often seen as a spiritual misalignment first.

The Environment

So taking it a step further now we understand this *'Mirror Effect'*, we look at the environment around us and learn to observe our individual and collective reflection in the world around. This is also closely related to what is called *"Law of Attraction"* or vibration/energetic alignment. The most important thing to remember is that what we observe and experience is the result of our inner state and this is purely within our domain. We reap and harvest according to our own character and our innermost desires - it is this that we manifest!

> *"whatsoever a man sows, that shall he also reap."*
>
> *Galatians 6:7 LAMSA*

and

> *"So every good tree bears good fruits; but a bad tree bears bad fruits."*
>
> *Matthew 7:17 LAMSA*

According to Swedenborg our surroundings appear according to one's inner state, although in the spiritual realm much more swiftly and directly than in the natural world, due to the harmony and similarity of character in each community. (e.g. see *Heaven and Hell* 87-115 and 172-175)

We may be looking to the outside to be rescued and hope that attending church or prayer circles may heal, but ultimately it is our innermost desires and nature that needs to change:

> "God, who made the world and everything in it, since He is Lord of heaven and earth, does not dwell in temples made with hands."
>
> Acts 17:24 NKJV

The idea that our life experience and the environment we live in reflect our spirit is pervasive across many cultures. One example is the Shinto indigenous spiritual tradition (Japan) who believe that pollution of spirit (*kegare*) leads to disorder in environment, while purity leads to natural harmony. In other words, the environment mirrors our interior state.

Our Regeneration

So far we discussed the order of creation: from the Divine source down to the 'external' environment that reflects us. Ultimately the path to health is through alignment with the Divine Order: by accepting what is good and true, aligning our heart and mind. Meaning in the simplest of terms: a healthy mind means a healthy body.

The awareness of the creation process and correspondence of the external to what lies within will help align our natural life and so health to the perfect Divine order. Note, though, that we are imperfect, fallible and finite beings who experience a senses-based surrounding (ie space time) on account of our changing and imperfect natures. In other words, we are able to progress, learn and grow spiritually - becoming more whole and image of the perfect and infinite Source: Jehovah God.

This progress is also called spiritual reformation or regeneration, and is directly and intimately tied to our physical health journey too! It cannot be otherwise.

However, we have help - if we can accept it:

> "Behold, I make all things new."
>
> Revelation 21:5

> "A new heart also will I give you, and a new spirit will I put within you: and I will take away the stony heart out of your flesh, and I will give you an heart of flesh."
>
> Ezekiel 36:26

Swedenborg talks in length about the nature of God and our regeneration. While a bit of a larger excerpt, I think it is worth including these sections from his work *True Christian Religion* here:

> "What flows in from the Lord is received by man according to his form. Form means here man's state in respect both to his love and to his wisdom, consequently in respect both to his affections for the goods of charity and to his perceptions of the truths of faith.
> ...
> The life of God in all its fullness is not only in good and pious men, but also in the wicked and impious, likewise both in the angels of heaven and in the spirits of hell. The difference is that the wicked obstruct the way and close the door, lest God should enter the lower regions of their minds; while the good clear the way and open the door, and invite God to enter into the lower regions of their minds as he inhabits the highest regions; and thus they form a state of the will for love and charity to flow into, and a state of the understanding for wisdom and faith to flow into, consequently for the reception of God. But the wicked obstruct that influx by various lusts of the flesh and spiritual defilements, which bestrew the way and clog the passage."
>
> True Christian Religion 366 (Ager)

He continues further...

> "But the man who divides the Lord, charity, and faith, is not a form that receives but a form that destroys them.
> ...
> Charity is the essence of faith, and faith is the form of charity just as good is the essence of truth, and truth is the form of good. As there are these two, namely, good and truth, in each thing and in all things that have essential existence, so there are charity and faith, charity because it belongs to good, and faith because it belongs to truth. This may be illustrated by comparisons with many things in the human body, and with many things on the earth."
>
> True Christian Religion 367 (Ager)

This process is all about the (re)alignment of our spirit (ie our loves and understanding) to the perfect source: all that is good and true.

The path Buddha taught is called the *Noble Eightfold Path* to follow: right understanding, intention, speech, action, livelihood, effort, mindfulness and concentration.

The Bhagavad Gītā highlights that surrender to the Divine restores harmony and liberation as the Divine descends to restore "dharma" (cosmic order). (eg 4.7–8, 18.66)

The Qur'ān tells us that God invites all who have transgressed to return and that He "restores." That a process of purification and divine mercy restore one's state. (eg 24:21, 39:53)

The idea of realignment with the Creator and life force, by right living (ie living what is good and true) - then restoring harmony and health is very common in many indigenous traditions too. For example in Māori tradition it is called *Whakapai / Mauri Ora* —concept of realignment with life-force restores health and harmony.

It is exactly this process of restoration/regeneration/reformation of the human spirit that is the goal of spirituality and the reason for our creation and life experience. The good news is that while we are here, and have capacity to think, we can grow and improve our mental and physical health. The caveat is that it is our personal responsibility, given that nothing can force you to believe, feel or think anything - you are the captain of your own mind!

Summary

One law of order operates reality through correspondences; every level reflects and sustains the one above it. Divine > Spiritual/Mental > Natural/Bodily. Healing, perception, and moral life are one continuum. Across Christian, Hindu, Islamic, and Indigenous traditions, the teachings are remarkably similar when you analyse them:

- There is one Divine source
- There is an unseen causal realm
- The mind connects spirit and body
- The natural world is a manifestation
- The body mirrors inner states
- The environment reflects consciousness
- Regeneration restores harmony with Divine order

This is about as close to a universal spiritual pattern as we find in comparative theology. In modern scientific consideration, quantum physics and the elaboration of reality collapsing from a quantum field (metaphysical source) at point of observation (consciousness) - eerily describes what we can learn from all these sources and other mystics: we manifest reality through thought, with everything grounded in a single infinite consciousness.

To put it into different words:

> "Therefore, I say to you, all things for which you pray and ask, believe that you have received them, and they will be granted to you."
>
> Mark 11:24 NASB

> "Truly, truly I say to you, if you ask the Father for anything in My name, He will give it to you."
>
> John 16:23 NASB

In plain language: we are always granted that which we want if we are sincere enough and expect it. This is a universal law, often referred to as the "*Law of Attraction*". To put it even more simple - we manifest and attract that what we love - God **always** gives us what we truly love, but without overriding our and others' freewill:

> "Let it be as you desire."
>
> Matthew 15:28

It is therefore critically important to be aware of what we are focusing our attention and energy on, subconsciously and consciously. Since we do, to put it in a different way: fulfil our own prophesies - we must be very careful about what we wish for and how we 'see' our future be. What is the future you want to manifest?

See also: Matthew 21:22, John 14:13-14, John 15:7, James 1:5-6, Matthew 7:7, Philipians 4:6, 1 John 3:22, Matthew 18:19, 1 john 5:14-15

The Healing Process

*I*t should be very obvious now that it is vital for change to occur that it comes from a place of deep personal commitment: consciously and subconsciously so. For the mind and body to change, the heart must change and be open. Therefore we must commit and open our heart to accept what is good and true until it becomes second nature.

False thinking, and living contrary to what is objectively true leads to frustration, disappointment, stress and disease. We must be guided by wisdom through logic and rationality. We only free our mind and become open to change when we accept reality.

What we think (believe) and feel (love) are in themselves imaginary concepts. They must be applied and practised. Only when what is good and true are accepted and integrated in life do they manifest and can we benefit from the progressive alignment with reality that follows.

When our minds operate in harmony with the flow and fundamental laws of creation, no disease state can exist. All disorder (disease) is the result of this flow being impeded, which occurs as a result of false and limited thinking and desires.

> "Go your way; and as you have believed, so let it be done for you."
>
> Matthew 8:13

because:

> "...all things are possible to him who believes."
>
> Mark 9:23

How to use this book

*D*aily healing sessions can be performed in different ways, there isn't one way more effective than another, as long as the recipient is willing to receive healing, both consciously and sub-consciously! They can be mixed and don't always need to be in same place connections over the phone or video conference will also be supportive, because the realm of intention, which is the realm of causation, is outside of space time.

Group Sessions
Within the presence of a church pastor and/or elders form a circle around the healing recipient. Before commencing, it will be good for the whole group to be aligned and focused, which can be done by sharing in the Lord's Prayer.

At least the person who is leading the prayer should put one hand on the recipient if possible, other members may form concentric circles or hold hands.

The leader will read out the scripture texts, affirmations (which are to be repeated by the recipient) and then the prayer.

During the session, the recipient may also be anointed with a small drop of oil on the forehead, for example holy frankincense.

The most important aspect is the focus and sincerity of intention of the group and recipient, so it is best to avoid possible distractions - like making sure phones are silent and there is a little privacy.

Couple Sessions

In a home setting, or via phone or video-conferencing, a partner can assist with leading the session. Laying on of hands will help and anointing with oil may be less convenient or common, but still optional if the recipient is accepting. In such private setting, hands may be laid on or hover a little above the site needing healing and the crown of the head.

The healing recipient must verbalise / sincerely acknowledge the affirmations and read out the prayer. It is important to own the affirmations and to believe they are true.

Private Personal Sessions

This may include some prerecorded messages of support or prayer that the healing recipient can listen to. In this scenario, the healing recipient simply reads and reflects on the day's scripture, affirmations and prayer themselves.

It is important that as a healing recipient, you quiet the mind and minimise any possible interruptions or distractions. Prepare as you would for any reflective prayer or meditation session.

After the upcoming 30 days of healing prayer sessions has been completed, you may decide to continue with another cycle, especially for more chronic and complex health issues which take a bit more time to heal.

Remember that healing is often not instantaneous, but a process. It takes as long as it takes for us to let go and change that which is ultimately causing it. This is frequently some form of trauma, resentment or fear - something no longer serving us, but consciously or subconsciously we still hold onto it.

Daily Healing Sessions

"Behold, I give you the authority to trample on serpents and scorpions, and over all the power of the enemy, and nothing shall by any means hurt you!"

Luke 10:19 NKJV

The Lord's Prayer

Our Father in the heavens,
hallowed be your name.
Your kingdom come. Your will be done,
as in heaven, so upon the earth.
Give us today our daily bread.
And forgive us our debts,
as we also forgive our debtors.
And do not lead us into temptation,
but deliver us from evil.
For yours is the kingdom
and the power and the glory, for ever.
Amen

Daily proclamation:

Through my faith in His name: I am Now healthy. I am Now free. I am Now healed. It is done Right Now, in Jesus Name! Every day, I become healthier and healthier, stronger and stronger, younger and younger! Because the Word of God, working mightily in my body, Now!

"Let it be as you desire."

Matthew 15:28

Day 1

The Lord is my healer

"I am the Lord who heals you."
Exodus 15:26 NKJV

"Bless the Lord, O my soul, and forget not all His benefits: Who forgives all your iniquities, who heals all your diseases."
Psalm 103:2-3 LAMSA

"the Lord will take away from you all sickness."
Deuteronomy 7:15 NKJV

Confessions/Affirmations

- I accept my healing and reject all fear
- I believe God's word is true and He is healing me right now
- I accept that with God all things are possible
- I will prosper in perfect health

Prayer

Heavenly Father, thank you for my recovery and healing and giving me the strength and courage each day in this journey. Thank you for forgiving me, so I can let go of guilt or shame.

Day 2

God's word never fails

"So will My word be which goes out of My mouth; It will not return to Me empty, Without accomplishing what I desire, And without succeeding in the purpose for which I sent it."
Isaiah 55:11 NASB

"For with God nothing shall be impossible."
Luke 1:37

"He sent His word and healed them, and delivered them from their destructions."
Psalm 107:20 NKJV

Confessions/Affirmations
- I trust the Word of God fully
- I accept He is healing me right now
- I accept that with God all things are possible
- I put more trust in God than in the opinions of people

Prayer
Heavenly Father, thank you for your Word and delivering me from sickness. I thank you for being faithful and true. Help me to keep my eyes on your promise.

Day 3

God gives power and strength without fail

"He gives power to the weary, and to them that are stricken with disease* he increases strength."
                              Isaiah 40:29 LAMSA
                    *(also translated as weak or powerless)

"Jesus Christ is the same yesterday, today, and forever."
                              Hebrews 13:8 NKJV

Confessions/Affirmations

- I have access to infinite healing power
- I trust that God always gives me the strength I need, when I need it
- Jesus Christ is healing me today and will always be healing those in need
- I know and accept that God restores me daily

Prayer

Heavenly Father, thank you for restoring me and giving me the power to heal minute by minute, day by day. Inside and out. I am glad to know you are continuously renewing my heart, mind, and body.

Day 4

With God everything is possible

> *"And one of them struck the servant of the high priest and cut off his right ear. But Jesus answered and said, "Permit even this." And He touched his ear and healed him."*
>
> Luke 22:50-51 NKJV

> *"But Jesus looked at them and said, 'With men it is impossible, but not with God; for with God all things are possible.'"*
>
> Mark 10:27 NKJV

Confessions/Affirmations

- I accept Divine Healing in my life, right now
- I believe everything is possible with God
- I know that Jesus restores me completely whole, if I let Him
- I know and trust that my healing is happening now

Prayer

Dear Lord, I know you can restore me fully regardless of doctor's opinions. I accept you in my life and thank you for the healing that is happening right now. I know everything is possible with you!

Day 5

Full authority is His and yours

"Then Jesus came to them and said, 'All authority in heaven and on earth has been given to me.'"
Matthew 28:18-19

"Behold, I give you the authority to trample on serpents and scorpions, and over all the power of the enemy, and nothing shall by any means hurt you."
Luke 10:19 NKJV

Confessions/Affirmations
- I know Jesus has full authority on earth and over any disease
- I know that through Jesus I too have power over the enemy
- I trust that nothing shall hurt me in Jesus name
- I believe I can defeat this illness or disease

Prayer

Dear Jesus Christ, Heavenly Father. Thank you for giving me the power and authority needed to overcome this world and to defeat the enemy. You are my refuge and strength.

Day 6

Joyfulness is healing

"A joyful heart is good medicine, but a broken spirit dries up the bones."
Proverbs 17:22 NASB

"Do not sorrow, for the joy of the Lord is your strength."
Nehemiah 8:10 NKJV

Confessions/Affirmations
- I let go of fear, judgement and worry and accept joy in my life
- I am filled with joy and peace believing in the promise of The Word
- The joy of the Lord is my strength, there is no place for sorrow
- I am filled with abundance and healing through the fullness of God

Prayer
Dear Lord, you love and give without reserve to everyone. Thank you for your compassion and healing and giving me the strength to face each day anew with joy and the power to cast aside my worries, pain and sense of loss. I hand it all to you.

Day 7

Wait on The Lord for renewal

"But those who wait on the LORD Shall renew their strength; They shall mount up with wings like eagles, They shall run and not be weary, They shall walk and not faint."

Isaiah 40:31 NKJV

"He heals the brokenhearted and binds up their wounds."

Psalm 147:3 NASB

Confessions/Affirmations

- I am being renewed each moment by the perfect love of God
- I know I am clean through the spoken Word
- I let go of insecurity, sorrow, fear and anxiety: I accept the wings of strength from the Lord today
- I refuse to give up and be defeated. Sickness will flee from me and victory belongs to me now!

Prayer

Holy Heavenly Father, Thank you for giving me strength to follow the path you set before me. I know you guide me to wholeness and renewal of heart, mind and body.

Day 8

The Lord gives you abundant life

"The thief comes only to steal and kill and destroy; I came so that they would have life, and have it abundantly."
John 10:10 NASB

"There shall no evil befall you, neither shall any plague come near your dwelling."
Psalm 91:10 LAMSA

Confessions/Affirmations
- I am delivered and protected from destructive forces
- I know the Word is life and health to my flesh
- I accept abundance and joy in my life right now
- I place full trust in You Lord, so I will not be swayed by the illusions of this world. I reject all lies of the devil.

Prayer
Dear Lord, you heal me from my brokenness and lead me on the path of righteousness. Thank you for protecting me and giving me life in abundance.

Day 9

You shall prosper

"No weapon formed against you shall prosper."
Isaiah 54:17 NKJV

"I will give you the keys of the kingdom of heaven; and whatever you bind on earth shall be bound in heaven, and whatever you release on earth shall be released in heaven."
Matthew 16:19 LAMSA

Confessions/Affirmations

- I have the keys and accept my given power to bind my spirit and body to love, truth and healing
- I let go of selfish attitudes, destructive habits, fear and helplessness - I am free to make my own choices
- I am healed, strengthened and comforted in your Word
- I can do all things in Christ, who lives in me

Prayer

Dear Lord, thank you for giving me courage and wisdom to face this journey and follow your path of love and truth. I surrender any obstacles to my healing and prosperity in life. Thank you for loving me

Day 10

You will be healed

"'For I will restore you to health And I will heal you of your wounds,' declares the LORD."
Jeremiah 30:17 NASB

"But when Jesus saw her, He called her to Him and said to her, 'Woman, you are loosed from your infirmity.'"
Luke 13:12 NKJV

Confessions/Affirmations
- I have been set free from my wounds, physical and mental
- I accept healing is happening now, inside and outside
- Jesus is my Healer, there is no more powerful force
- I am filled with God's healing power and authority

Prayer
Lord Jesus, sickness, disease and brokenness are not your wish for me. I thank you for helping me in times of uncertainty, unbelief and doubt when my health is failing. I accept your mercy and grace and focus on your unfailing promise.

Day 11

In His name you are protected

"And these signs will follow those who believe: In My name they will cast out demons; they will speak with new tongues; they will take up serpents; and if they drink anything deadly, it will by no means hurt them; they will lay hands on the sick, and they will recover."
Mark 16:17-18 NKJV

"Thus says the LORD God to these bones: Behold, I will cause breath to enter into you, and you shall live."
Ezekiel 37:5 LAMSA

Confessions/Affirmations
- In His name I am protected and the sick recover
- I receive the breath of life, sickness has no place in His name
- I look at life with renewed hope and vision
- In the name of Jesus, I am protected, free and healthy!

Prayer

Heavenly Father, thank you for my life and protection against demonic forces. Life and healing only come from you. Your healing hand ensures my full recovery.

Day 12

Peace and strength is yours

"Behold, I will bring it health and cure; I will cure them and reveal unto them the abundance of peace and truth."
Jeremiah 33:6

"I will seek that which was lost, and bring again that which was driven away, and will bind up that which was broken, and will strengthen that which was sick"
Ezekiel 34:16

Confessions/Affirmations
- I am completely at peace
- My health and healing is being revealed day by day
- My strength is returning evermore each day
- I can do all things in Christ who strengthens me

Prayer
Lord, all things are possible with You. Thank you for giving me strength and peace along my journey to recovery. You sustain and renew me continuously. You only bring me healing without judgment.

Day 13

He heals everyone

"And the whole multitude sought to touch Him, for power went out from Him and healed them all."
Luke 6:19 NKJV

"But just say the word, and my servant will be healed."
Luke 7:7 NASB

Confessions/Affirmations
- I belief the Word is true and His power is real
- By His Word and power I am healed
- God wants me well. Jesus came, so that I might have life and that I might have it more abundantly!
- His Healing is without reservation available to everyone

Prayer
Dear Lord Jesus, Heavenly Father, in Your name I release the stronghold of this disease and let it go. I only accept love, peace and healing power. Thank you for your Word.

Day 14

The Lord heals every kind of disease

> *"And standing over her, He rebuked the fever, and it left her; and she immediately got up and served them."*
>
> Luke 4:39 NASB

> *"Now when the sun was setting, all they that had any sick with diverse diseases brought them unto him; and he laid his hands on every one of them, and healed them."*
>
> Luke 4:40

Confessions/Affirmations

- I know my disease can be overcome, there is no disease impossible for Him
- His hands are constantly on my shoulders, giving me courage, strength and healing
- Even when I am momentarily weak, He lifts and protects me
- His healing power surrounds me every moment

Prayer

Dear God, I place hope and trust in Your promises. Your Word is true. Therefore healing is mine if I want it. Thank you for giving me the wisdom and will to fulfil Your purpose for me.

Day 15

The Spirit of God heals all sickness

"When Jesus saw her, He called her over and said to her, 'Woman, you are freed from your sickness.'"
Luke 13:12 NASB

"And there was a man before him, who had dropsy.... So he took him, and healed him, and let him go."
Luke 14:2,4 LAMSA

"But you are not in the flesh but in the Spirit, if indeed the Spirit of God dwells in you. Now if anyone does not have the Spirit of Christ, he is not His. And if Christ is in you, the body is dead because of sin, but the Spirit is life because of righteousness. But if the Spirit of Him who raised Jesus from the dead dwells in you, He who raised Christ from the dead will also give life to your mortal bodies through His Spirit who dwells in you."
Romans 8:9-11 NKJV

Confessions/Affirmations

- I know the Spirit of God dwells in me: Christ is in me
- This same spirit releases the bonds of my disease and heals me
- I receive the gift of life every single moment anew
- Through speaking, laying on of hand and any other way that I choose to let the power flow, I release the power of God

Prayer

Dear Lord, Heavenly Father. Thank for for opening my eyes to see the beauty and life I receive continuously from You. Your Spirit brings life and purpose and healing and joy will be the result that manifests.

Day 16

The Lord has overcome the world

> *"These things I have spoken to you so that in Me you may have peace. In the world you have tribulation, but take courage; I have overcome the world."*
>
> John 16:33 NASB

> *"But you are of God, my children, and have overcome them: because he who is among you is greater than he who is in the world."*
>
> 1 John 4:4 LAMSA

> *"When evening had come, they brought to Him many who were demon-possessed. And He cast out the spirits with a word, and healed all who were sick, that it might be fulfilled which was spoken by Isaiah the prophet, Saying:'He Himself took our infirmities and bore our sicknesses.'"*
>
> Matthew 8:16-17 NKJV

Confessions/Affirmations

- I am in Christ and through the Holy Spirit am set free from the powers of this world
- I know the life of the Holy Spirit is filling and renewing all my cells right now
- I reject sickness and sin: in the name of Jesus Christ, I am delivered from sickness and sin right now!
- My body is filled with life and health

Day 16

Prayer

Dear Lord, You have overcome the natural and worldy powers of illusion. Thank you for helping me do the same in Your Spirit and removing my sickness and disease.

Day 17

You are healed and delivered

"Is anyone among you sick? Let him call for the elders of the church, and let them pray over him, anointing him with oil in the name of the Lord. And the prayer of faith will save the sick, and the Lord will raise him up. And if he has committed sins, he will be forgiven. Confess your trespasses to one another, and pray for one another, that you may be healed. The effective, fervent prayer of a righteous man avails much."

James 5:14-16 NKJV

"He sent out his word and healed them, and delivered them from their destruction."

Psalms 107:20

Confessions/Affirmations
- I forbid and bind all works of the devil now!
- I accept forgiveness and forgive myself
- The Holy Spirit is healing me as we speak
- I refuse any sickness or disease to stay in my body

Prayer

Thank you Lord Jesus for my delivery and healing. If I remain in you no sickness and disease can remain. I love you and am grateful for your grace and mercy.

Day 18

Freely you receive

> "As you go, proclaim this message: 'The kingdom of heaven has come near.' Heal the sick, raise the dead, cleanse those who have leprosy, drive out demons. Freely you have received; freely give."
>
> Matthew 10:7-8

> "Then your light will break out like the dawn, And your recovery will speedily spring forth; And your righteousness will go before you; The glory of the LORD will be your rear guard."
>
> Isaiah 58:8 NASB

Confessions/Affirmations

- I am filled with the Holy Spirit and His Power!
- I know and I believe right now that the power of the Holy Spirit is flowing out from my spirit, filling every cell of my body - casting out all sicknesses, casting out all infirmities and all demonic influences over the mind
- No sickness, no disease and no death can touch my body, I am full with life, because the Spirit of God dwells in me!
- He who is in me, is greater than all the sicknesses and diseases! I am free.

Prayer

Dear God, I know you are The Healer and nothing compares with your might and power. I thank you for my healing and for nourishing my soul and mind. Thank you for giving me each day what I need.

Day 19

Healing the multitudes

"And Jesus went forth, and saw a great multitude, and was moved with compassion toward them, and he healed their sick."

Matthew 14:14

"And Jesus went about all Galilee, teaching in their synagogues, and preaching the gospel of the kingdom, and healing all manner of sickness and all manner of disease among the people."

Matthew 4:23

Confessions/Affirmations

- I know God freely gives me all things: I freely receive life and health
- I am delivered from all sickness and disease, pain and mental torment!
- I known that by Jesus all my problems are solved
- I can endure and complete this healing journey - God gives me the strength I need

Prayer

Jesus Christ, Heavenly Father, thank you for your compassion and healing: For making me healthier, stronger and younger each day and each moment. You never fail.

Day 20

Sickness will be removed

"But you shall serve the Lord your God, and He will bless your bread and your water; and I will remove sickness from your midst."

Exodus 23:25 NASB

"But he was slain for our sins, he was afflicted for our iniquities; the chastisement of our peace was upon him, and with his wounds we are healed."

Isaiah 53:5 LAMSA

Confessions/Affirmations

- I know Jesus loves me and blesses me and will remove any infirmity, disease or illness.
- I have been delivered from all sickness and disease, mental and physical.
- I am set free: right now, I am healed!
- I know that He who is in me is truly greater than any sickness or disease!

Prayer

In your holy name Lord Jesus Christ, I command every illegal invasion of sickness to leave me immediately. I thank you Heavenly Father for sustaining and uplifting me in health, joy and peace. Amen

Day 21

The Lord is willing - always!

"And it happened when He was in a certain city, that behold, a man who was full of leprosy saw Jesus; and he fell on his face and implored Him, saying, 'Lord, if You are willing, You can make me clean.' Then He put out His hand and touched him, saying, 'I am willing; be cleansed.' Immediately the leprosy left him."
Luke 5:12-13 NKJV

"And if the Spirit of Him who raised our LORD Jesus Christ from the dead dwells within you, so he who raised Jesus Christ from the dead will also quicken your mortal bodies by his Spirit that dwells within you."
Romans 8:11 LAMSA

Confessions/Affirmations

- I know the Spirit who raised Jesus from the dead lives in me. The Spirit within me is greater than all the evils in the world
- Because of His Holy Spirit, I have every blessing and answer to every problem!
- I believe the Word of God, which tells me The Lord is always willing to heal: through my faith I am healed
- I am a person of faith, and through faith and patience I inherit all His promises

Prayer

Dear God, Thank you for your unceasing love and wisdom. Thank you for your unceasing power and authority over disorder, chaos, disease, anxiety and all other afflictions from the devil. Your healing power reigns supreme.

Day 22

The name of Jesus has authority

> *"Now, Lord, look on their threats, and grant to Your servants that with all boldness they may speak Your word, by stretching out Your hand to heal, and that signs and wonders may be done through the name of Your holy Servant Jesus."*
>
> Acts 4:29-30 NKJV

> *"And every man was seized with amazement, and spoke among themselves, saying, What kind of word is this, that he commands unclean spirits with authority and power, and they go out!"*
>
> Luke 4:36 LAMSA

Confessions/Affirmations

- In the name of Jesus I have every spiritual blessing in the heavenly realms, right now!
- I reject every lie of the enemy and every form of lacking
- I walk in the power and authority of Jesus Christ, because I am in Him and He in me
- I know that I am blessed, healthy, and prosperous

Prayer

Jesus Christ, Heavenly Father, Jehovah God, King of the Universe. Thank you for my life, thank you for looking after my eternal welfare in every single moment, thank you for my daily blessings and providing for everything I need in every single moment.

Day 23

He bore our sins

"And he bore all our sins, and lifted them with his body on the cross, that we being dead to sin, should live through his righteousness: and by his wounds you were healed."
1 Peter 2:24 LAMSA

"And they lifted up their voices and said, 'Jesus, Master, have mercy on us!' So when He saw them, He said to them, 'Go, show yourselves to the priests.' And so it was that as they went, they were cleansed."
Luke 17:13-14 NKJV

Confessions/Affirmations

- I know that I am forgiven each moment anew, because in Him I am created anew in each moment - I too release the past completely
- I believe that Jesus, The Word, came to heal us, and that He came to deliver us from death
- I trust the Word of God because the Word of God has real power and authority! - and with God nothing shall be impossible!

Prayer

Dear Jesus, thank you for filling every cell in my body with life and health. Thank you for cleansing me and driving out all sickness, weakness, doubt and fear. In you I have hope, peace, joy and complete health. Amen

Day 24

Have faith and receive

"What do you want Me to do for you?" He said, "Lord, that I may receive my sight." Then Jesus said to him, "Receive your sight; your faith has made you well."
Luke 18:41-42 NKJV

"And He said to her, 'Daughter, be of good cheer; your faith has made you well. Go in peace.'"
Luke 8:48 NKJV

Confessions/Affirmations
- I have faith in the Word of God and in the promise of healing
- Through faith I am healed, from head to toe I am restored
- I command my body to line up with the Word of God and to be healed and restored to full health
- I will enjoy life, be cheerful and have peace, knowing that I am made well

Prayer

Jehovah God, thank you for your healing. Thank you for your peace. No disease or illness is to difficult for you to overcome. In your name I am healed right now. Thank you.

Day 25

The Lord will preserve you

"The LORD will preserve him and keep him alive, and he shall bless him upon the earth; he will not deliver him into the hands of his enemies. The LORD will strengthen him upon his sick bed; he will wholly recover from his illness."

Psalm 41:2-3 LAMSA

"so that handkerchiefs or aprons were even carried from his body to the sick, and the diseases left them and the evil spirits went out."

Acts 19:12 NASB

Confessions/Affirmations

- I submit myself to God and use the Word to resist the devil and his lies
- I know that the Lord will preserve me and bless me with a healthy life
- I know the Word is more powerful than a piece of cloth, so disease cannot remain in me
- I believe the promise of God over the opinions of man

Prayer

Dear Lord, I know that whatever is born of God overcomes the world. And my faith is the victory that has also overcome the world. By your Word I am preserved. Amen

Day 26

Submit yourselves, take refuge

"The Lord also will be a refuge for the oppressed, a refuge in times of trouble. And those who know Your name will put their trust in You; for You, Lord, have not forsaken those who seek You."

Psalm 9:9-10 NKJV

"Submit yourselves therefore to God. Resist the devil, and he will flee from you."

James 4:7

Confessions/Affirmations

- God is with me. He is the Light. In Him there is no darkness at all.
- I take refuge in the name of Jesus Christ, which is above all the names of every sicknesses!
- I have authority to tread on serpents and scorpions and over all the power of the enemy!
- Therefore, in the name of Jesus, all illegal invasions of darkness; Right now I command you to cease from my body! All sicknesses, depression and infirmity, I command you, now you must leave me!

Prayer

Dear Lord, Jehovah God in you I place my life and trust. Because of you I am able to stand tall, reject evil and disorder from my body and take shelter in your name. My health is being fully restored now. Amen

Day 27

You have the spirit of power and love

> *"Then the eyes of the blind will be opened and the ears of the deaf will be unstopped. Then the lame will leap like a deer, and the tongue of the mute will shout for joy."*
> Isaiah 35:5-6 NASB

> *"For God has not given us a spirit of fear, but of power and of love and of a sound mind."*
> 2 Timothy 1:7 NKJV

Confessions/Affirmations
- I surrender to love and joy, I reject all fear
- I continue to look to life with hope and optimism, believing every moment the Lord is guiding me to a life filled with more hope, health and joy
- I know God is moment by moment, cell by cell, giving me the gift of a sound mind and sound body
- I am not weak, but have power. I have no fear, but hope. I have no pain, but joy. I have no anger, but love.

Prayer
Dear Lord Jesus, Thank you for your love, compassion and truth. Through your power I am made well and am restored in mind and body: inside and out.

Day 28

It is never too late

"Then He came and touched the open coffin, and those who carried him stood still. And He said, 'Young man, I say to you, arise.' So he who was dead sat up and began to speak. And He presented him to his mother."
Luke 7:14-15 NKJV

"But He put them all outside, took her by the hand and called, saying, 'Little girl, arise.' Then her spirit returned, and she arose immediately."
Luke 8:54 NKJV

"And as he brought him, the demon attacked him and convulsed him. And Jesus rebuked the unclean spirit, and healed the boy, and gave him to his father."
Luke 9:42 LAMSA

Confessions/Affirmations

- I know time is an illusion and to Him who is without time, change is never too late
- I am filled with life, filled with the life of Christ
- I am filled with supernatural healing and divine health
- I know my spirit is strong within me and I have eternal life

Day 28

Prayer

Heavenly Father, sickness and disease is not your will for me or anyone. Thank you for loving me and making me whole. I thank you for giving me the faith and strength, daily.

Day 29

You will live a long life

"O LORD my God, I cried to You for help, and You healed me."

Psalm 30:2 NASB

"And the LORD said, 'My spirit shall not always strive with man, for that he also is flesh: yet his days shall be an hundred and twenty years.'"

Genesis 6:3

"With a long life I will satisfy him And let him see My salvation."

Psalm 91:16 NASB

Confessions/Affirmations
- I know in Christ I have eternal life
- I believe God is protecting me and guiding me, caring for my eternal welfare.
- I live by the law of the Spirit of life, and have through the Word overcome the law of sin and death!
- Therefore, every cell in my body is full with life and power!

Day 29

Prayer

Jesus Christ, our Heavenly Father. I thank you that you command my body to be restored, to be healed, to be full with life and be in full health - and thank you for giving me the authority to do the same!

Day 30

Do not be afraid

"I shall not die, but live, and declare the works of the Lord."

Psalm 118:17 NKJV

"Do not fear, for I am with you; Do not be afraid, for I am your God. I will strengthen you, I will also help you, I will also uphold you with My righteous right hand."

Isaiah 41:10 NASB

"Seek the LORD and you shall live;"

Amos 5:6 LAMSA

Confessions/Affirmations

- I know I have been delivered from all kinds of sicknesses and diseases in this very moment!
- Right Now, I am healed and I live in divine health
- I know God strengthens me each moment, so I reject all fear: God is in my corner, I shall not be afraid
- I declare the works of the Lord and shall live!

Prayer

Dear Lord, Jehovah God, I look forward to life with hope and optimism, knowing I am completely set free and restored to good health in your name! I freely receive your love, peace and joy - which I also share with all those around me.

The Word

When people hear the phrase *The Word*, most instinctively think of the Bible. Some even consider the printed book itself to be sacred in and of its pages, as if the physical ink on its physical paper held some kind of supernatural essence.

But I suggest it to you that The Word is not the Bible - and the Bible is not The Word.

Certainly, the Bible is a vessel — a finite container, if you will — that holds a representation of the Word, but The Word, in its truest and most complete sense, is far more expansive. It is nothing less than what is of the Divine itself.

> *"In the beginning was the Word, and the Word was with God, and the Word was God."*
>
> *John 1:1*

> *"God is reality itself, and everything that exists must come from that reality."*
>
> *Divine Love and Wisdom 55*

Swedenborg tells us that "the Word" signifies Divine Truth — not just truth as a concept, but Truth as the very structure of all being.

He writes:

> *"The Word is Divine truth itself, thus the Lord Himself. For the Lord is the Word because He is the Divine truth, and the Word is the Divine truth because it is from the Lord and concerning the Lord."*
>
> *Doctrine of the Sacred Scripture 1*

This means that everything which is in harmony with what is good and true - everything that arises from Divine Love and expresses Divine Wisdom — is the Word. The Word is the form, or structure, which Love takes when it manifests as thought, reason, creation, and purposeful order. It is the Divine intelligibility behind all things.

To say it plainly: The Word is reality itself — the Divine order, purpose, and wisdom from which and by which all things exist and continue to be.

.... read the full chapter in *New Perspectives*

Prayer

*P*eople often think of prayer as words—carefully chosen phrases, set forms, or spontaneous petitions. But I put it to you that prayer, in its essence, is not firstly what we say; it is what we will.

True prayer is a wishing—an interior desire aimed at something. As such, prayer is intimately the same as loving. Our love is our will, and what we most deeply will is what we are forever "saying" to heaven with or without our lips.

> *"for your Father knows the things you have need of before you ask Him."*
>
> Matthew 6:8

Swedenborg is unambiguous about the primacy of the will (love) over mere speech:

> *"The love in the will is the end in view, and in the understanding it seeks and finds causes through which it may advance to its realisation."*
>
> True Christian Religion 658

A person's life is therefore the shape of their love and if love is the end we continually pursue, then prayer—being what we wish for (or will)—is with us constantly. It follows that we are always praying, because we are always willing.

.... read the full chapter in *New Perspectives*

What we cannot control

We have read how the natural world, and so our bodies, are a reflection of the spiritual and more specifically, our inner nature or character - what we love. This is true, it cannot be otherwise, since this is the underpinning nature and fundamental law of reality. However, it is important to provide some further context to avoid leaving you - my dear reader - with the singular impression that we are always and fully in control or responsible for our states and so our disease or illness. This is definitely not the case: at many times we are certainly so, but not always. The scriptures attest to this too:

> *"Now as Jesus passed by, He saw a man who was blind from birth. And His disciples asked Him, saying, 'Rabbi, who sinned, this man or his parents, that he was born blind?' Jesus answered, 'Neither this man nor his parents sinned, but that the works of God should be revealed in him. I must work the works of Him who sent Me while it is day; the night is coming when no one can work. As long as I am in the world, I am the light of the world.'*
>
> *When He had said these things, He spat on the ground and made clay with the saliva; and He anointed the eyes of the blind man with the clay. And He said to him, 'Go, wash in the pool of Siloam' (which is translated, Sent). So he went and washed, and came back seeing."*
>
> John 9:1-7 NKJV

(the term 'sin' should here be read as knowingly doing something wrong against the Divine Order.)

Why then was this person born blind? Why do children get sick? Why do we get sick besides the personal spiritual reasons already outlined? Here we learn about what I call a *'no fault clause'* and to understand my take on this there are a few factors you need to understand:

Firstly, and mercifully, the effect in the natural world does not show up immediately, but intermediately. The effect manifests with a delay in time. This delayed effect is the result of this natural realm being a shared stage displaying the collective and varying natures and so differing levels of alignment with the flow and fundamental laws of creation.

The main reason for this 'physical' realm is to provide us with some level of separation and freedom to explore our inner nature. This also enables us to experience a sense of autonomy, which is critical for our sense of self, which also allows us to experience the consequences or our states gently and progressively. And being a shared environment, we compete (for lack of a better term) with the causal effects of others' natures in the environment around us. This not only allows us, but even forces us, to reflect and consider our relationship with reality.

Could you imagine if you experienced the consequences of your thoughts and affections immediately without delay: being in a dreamlike state where everything constantly changes as your thinking shifts? You would have no freedom at all. While some people may suggest reality is individual and personal (solipsism), I don't believe that for many reasons: not in the least our lived experience.

Secondly, being spiritual beings we are connected. We are sensitive to, and influence, one another on the spiritual level. This unseen energetic sphere we call spiritual realm and science calls the quantum field, Lynne McTaggart simply calls *The Field*. We can tap into this *field*, which is done purposefully in with the process of muscle testing - popular in kineseology and other energetic healing modalities. David Hawkins describes it great detail in his book *Power vs Force*, a book I definitely recommend reading!

The out-take from this is that this field we are connected to affects us. In summary: Hawkins affirms that what is negative and false makes us inherently weak, while what is positive and true makes us strong. To say it differently, what is in order with the flow and fundamental laws of reality (creation) is strong, supportive and resilient, whereas that which is not, causes weakness and disorder.

Finally, we are not born a mindless drone or empty canvas. We are born with natures inherited from our parents and ancestors. This includes any associated innate character flaws and predispositions. Some of these give us extremely deep-rooted sensitivities and makes us prone to their (sometimes inevitable) effects. It is ourlife's journey, through introspection, to better ourselves, and so - hopefully - reduce the character flaws we ourselves pass down.

Interestingly Emanuel Swedenborg reveals that we receive our soul through the seed of our father - and with it therefore our deepest base nature, affections, disposition and inclinations. Incidentally too this shows up externally in our face. (Have you ever noticed that newborns tend to look a lot like their father?) In the womb this soul is 'clothed' with a body and takes on the more external predispositions and natures from both parents. (eg see *Divine Providence* 277, *Divine Love and Wisdom* 269 and *True Christian Religion* 103) It is also in the womb that our spiritual connections begin to form and energetic influence from the field and those around us. None of this we can actually influence ourselves - as fetus - at that time.

Before I go on, I think it also needs to be clearly understood that no illness should be judged or looked at from the lens of fault-finding. Neither blaming the 'victim' (patient) nor blaming ourselves and mull over the 'wouldv'es, couldv'es and shouldv'es is in any case helpful.

In any and all circumstance the focus should be on re-aligning ourselves with the Divine Order through deep personal introspection - a process we **ALL** should be doing regardless of our health and circumstance. We should focus on the positive options and steps we *can* take ourselves *now* to improve our own mental and physical health. It is not always wise to linger on the cause (or past): it is dangerous driving a car with eyes fixated on the rear-vision mirrors.

So, what does this mean? Why do we get sick or are in a state where we are more likely to become sick? Why do we find ourselves in these circumstances outside of our direct control or influence?

There is little one can do to reduce inherited predispositions to illness, especially as a child. As we mature we gain control over our impulses and inner life, allowing us consciously to challenge and curtail our predispositions. This only happens as we grow and learn about the nature of reality and our relationship with it. In context these two scriptures are then so important:

> *"But you seek first the kingdom of God and his righteousness, and all of these things shall be added to you."*
>
> Matthew 6:33 NKJV

> *"and you will know the truth, and the truth will set you free."*
>
> John 8:32 NASB

As parents, therefore, we can make sure we ourselves are as healthy mentally and physically as can be before having children. In the field of epi-genetics, it is well established that our genes (arguably the physical expression of our character and predispositions) are influenced by the mind: turning genes on or off and/or causing genetic mutations. There is no predetermination in the sense that makes us doomed. Having a particular cancer causing gene, for example, doesn't guarantee its expression and manifestation of tumours.

What we can be readily mindful of, as adults, is the influence of negativity and falsity, which has an effect on our physical and mental health. So keeping good company and avoid stress and negativity is always great advise. This includes books, music, television, work environments, family and neighbourhood environments and hobbies and personal interest aspects. Stress, negativity, antagonism, anger etc are toxic - politics is toxic, dark music is toxic - these energetically make you (and baby if pregnant) weaker and more prone to disease and illness.

This is also no different with exposure to environmental pollutants and toxins - they too operate on the energetic (spiritual) level to weaken us and impede the flow of creation in us. The same for drugs, poor diets and so forth. In the physical realm this usually shows up as inflammation or damage.

Luckily we can guard ourselves and build defences up against these negative influences. As you have read at the start of this book, you have been given the authority, strength, power and endurance to overcome them.

This only occurs through an introspective spiritual growth process (regeneration). Unfortunately this process is not quick - in the same way one cannot build a lot of muscle overnight. It is a lifelong process of continuous improvement, one we cannot truly begin until our late twenties. We can only truly change through freely choosing to change. By freely choosing to accept what is good and true. This change occurs one thought process at a time. I explain a little more about this in *New Perspectives*.

On the upside and seeing the blessings: disease or illness can be a great catalyst to force our focus and attention to this inner work and what is most important: our eternal life.

> *"True wisdom is seeing what is beneficial to your eternal life, and managing your life according to that. You do this when you not only know these things and grasp them with your understanding, but also will and do them."*
> Emanuel Swedenborg, Apocalypse Explained 338

* * *

Reference Sources

Scripture Sources

KJV   The Holy Bible, King James Version. Public Domain.

NKJV   The Holy Bible, New King James Version, Copyright © 1982 Thomas Nelson.

NASB   New American Standard Bible Copyright © 1960, 1962, 1963, 1968, 1971, 1972, 1973, 1975, 1977, 1995 by The Lockman Foundation, La Habra, Calif.

LAMSA   Holy Bible From The Ancient Eastern Texts: Aramaic Of The Peshitta by George M. Lamsa (1933). Public Domain.

References

Visser-Marchant, Cornelis. "New Perspectives: a fresh look at common spiritual topics." 2025, Freedom Philosophy, Australia. ISBN 978-0-6450743-4-5

Holz, Gary., Holz, Robbie. "Secrets of Aboriginal Healing: a physicist's journey with a remote Australian tribe" 2013, Bear & Company, Canada. ISBN 978-1-59143-175-6

Sant Singh Khalsa, MD. "Siri Guru Granth Sahib, Sentence by Sentence English Translation & Transliteration of." Available from https://www.khalsadarbar.com/PDFs/SriGuruGranthSahibJiDarpanEnglish.pdf (last accessed 22 November 2025)

Confucius (ca 500 BC). "The Doctrine of the Mean" available from The Internet Classics Archive by Daniel C. Stevenson: https://classics.mit.edu/Confucius/doctmean.html (last accessed 22 November 2025) English translator unknown.

Laozi/Lao-Tzu (老子) (4 BC) "Tao Te Ching" (道德经)

Available from World I-Kuan Tao Headquarters: https://www.with.org/tao_te_ching_en.pdf (last accessed 22 November 2025) English translator unknown.

Prabhupāda, A.C. Bhaktivedanta Swami. "Bhagavad-gītā As It Is" Second Edition, 1983 The Bhaktivedanta Book Trust International, Inc. ISBN: 978-0-89213-134-9

Swedenborg, Emanuel (1688-1772) "Divine Love and Wisdom" Standard Edition, Swedenborg Foundation 2009 Translated from the Original Latin by John C. Ager

Swedenborg, Emanuel (1688-1772) "Heaven and Its Wonders and Hell" Standard Edition, Swedenborg Foundation 2009 Translated from the Original Latin by John C. Ager

Swedenborg, Emanuel (1688-1772) "True Cristian Religion" Standard Edition, Swedenborg Foundation 2009 Translated from the Original Latin by John C. Ager

Swedenborg, Emanuel (1688-1772) "Arcana Coelestia" Standard Edition, Swedenborg Foundation 2009 Translated from the Original Latin by John Clowes, Revised and Edited by John Faulkner Potts

"The Holy Qur'ān" Arabic Text with English translation and short commentary. 2002 Islam International Publications Limited. ISBN: 978-1-85372-007-0

Inspiration drawn from

30 天医治之旅 ("*30 days declaration of healing Scriptures.*") 属天医治30天宣告(中英文).pdf: available from Dr Joyce Teh's website (康惠健康中心) https://gate-well.com/ (last accessed 16 November 2025) No author/publisher credits visible within the distributed PDF. Provenance review conducted on: 8 Nov 2025 (Australia/Brisbane)

Grow Churches (see https://growchurches.com/resources): *Healing Scriptures* compiled by Melanie Stone: available from https://growchurches.com/wp-content/uploads/2024/02/Healing-Scriptures.pdf (last accessed 16 November 2025)

Chuck and Joyce Baldwin (Father's House Church: https://www.fathershouse.org/) *30 Freedom Scriptures*: available from https://www.fathershouse.org/wp-content/uploads/2017/03/30-day-freedom-scriptures.pdf & *30 Days of Healing Prayer*: available from https://storage.cloversites.com/newhorizonchurch/documents/30days%20of%20healingprayer%2C%20format.pdf (last accessed 16 November 2025)

Pastor Nate Thompson's Deliverance Revolution Ministry: *Healing Prayers*: available from https://deliverancerevolution.org/prayers (last accessed 16 November 2025)

Becky Dvorak Healing And Miracles International. *100 Faith and Healing Scriptures*: available from https://authorbeckydvorak.com/wp-content/uploads/2018/03/100-faith-and-healing-scriptures.pdf (last accessed 16 November 2025)

Glenn Arekion Ministries: *Healing Confessions*: available from https://glennarekion.org/email_resources/Healing_Confessions.pdf (last accessed 16 November 2025)

Sandra Kennedy Ministries, The Healing Center (https://www.sandrakennedy.org/healing-center/): *Healing Scriptures*: available from https://www.sandrakennedy.org/wp-content/uploads/2024/02/Healing-Scriptures.pdf (last accessed 16 November 2025)

Possible Further Reading

Holz, Gary., Holz, Robbie. "Secrets of Aboriginal Healing: a physicist's journey with a remote Australian tribe" 2013, Bear & Company, Canada. ISBN 978-1-59143-175-6

Manickam, Chandrakumar. "Exercise Spiritual Authority." 2009, Creation House, US. ISBN: 978-1-59979-892-9

Goddard, Neville. "At Your Command." 2015, Watchmaker Publishing, US. ISBN: 978-1-60386-677-4 (Public Domain)

Goddard, Neville. "The Law and The Promise." 2023,

Reference Sources

Zincread. ISBN: 978-93-5740-065-7 (Public Domain)

Singh, Manhardeep. "12 Laws of the Universe." Self published. ISBN: 979-84-8234-859-8

Zeland, Vadim. "Transurfing in 78 Days: a practical course in creating your own reality." 2008, Ves Publishing, St Petersburg. ISBN: 978-5-9573-347-12

Visser-Marchant, Cornelis. "New Perspectives: a fresh look at common spiritual topics." 2025, Freedom Philosophy, Australia. ISBN 978-0-6450743-4-5

McTaggart, Lynne. "The Field: the quest for the secret force of the universe." Updated edition, 2008, HarperCollins, US. ISBN: 978-0-06-143518-8

Talbot, Michael. "The Holographic Universe." Reissued 2011, HarperCollins, US. ISBN: 978-0-06-201410-8

Hawkins, David R. "Power Vs Force: The Hidden Determinates of Human Behavior." 2014, Hay House Publishing, USA. ISBN: 978-14019450-7-7

Worcester, John. "Correspondences of the Bible: The Human Body." (originally published as Physiological Correspondences in 1889) Reprint 2009, Swedenborg Foundation, US. ISBN: 978-0-87785-114-1

Berridge, Norman J. "The Natural Basis of Spiritual Reality." 1993, Swedenborg Scientific Association, US. ISBN: 978-0-915221-69-1

Segal, Inna. "The Secret Language of Your Body." New revised, expanded and updated edition 2012, Blue Angel Publishing, Australia. ISBN: 978-0-9802865-5-7

Dispenza, Joe. "You Are the Placebo: making your mind matter." 5th edition, October 2018. Hay House. ISBN: 978-1-4019-4459-9

Tulk, Charles Augustus. "Spiritual Christianity Collected from the Theological Works of Emanuel Swedenborg." Originally published by William Newberry, London (1846) Reprint, Kessinger Publishing. ISBN: 978-0-548035-67-2 (public domain)

Other books by same author

New Perspectives
a fresh look at common spiritual topics

Daily Word
daily readings from The Word, with commentary and prayers by Reg Lang

Message in a Bottle
thoughts on classical liberalism and Australian politics

For more information:
www.freedomphilosophy.life

"..you shall know the truth, and the truth shall make you free."

John 8:32

Freedom Philosophy promotes a meaningful spirituality, teaching the essential practices of an effective spiritual life using ancient principles. When practised, these spiritual principles help us to free our minds, grow in wisdom, discover our purpose and strengthen our faith and connection with the Divine.

www.ingramcontent.com/pod-product-compliance
Lightning Source LLC
Chambersburg PA
CBHW031300290426
44109CB00012B/660